DOVER PERFORMANCE EDITION

Johannes Brahms

Complete Sonatas for Violin and Piano

With Separate Violin Part

Violin part edited by
LEOPOLD AUER

Piano part edited by
RUDOLPH GANZ

DOVER PUBLICATIONS, INC.
Mineola, New York

Bibliographical Note

This Dover edition, first published in 1996 and reprinted in 2012, is a new compilation in one volume of three sonatas by Johannes Brahms, originally published separately by Carl Fischer, New York, in the following editions of the Carl Fischer Music Library: Sonata No. 1 in G Major (No. L790, 1917); Sonata No. 2 in A Major (L791, n.d.); and Sonata No. 3 in D Minor (L792, 1916). The Dover edition adds a composite list of contents and movement numbers throughout.

International Standard Book Number

ISBN-13: 978-0-486-29312-7
ISBN-10: 0-486-29312-2

Manufactured in the United States by Courier Corporation
29312202
www.doverpublications.com

Contents

Three Sonatas for Violin and Piano

Sonata No. 1 in G Major
Op. 78 (1878–9)

I.

Adagio

III.

Allegro molto moderato

Sonata No. 2 in A Major

Op. 100 (1886)

I.

II.

III.

Allegretto grazioso (quasi Andante)

Sonata No. 3 in D Minor

Op. 108 (1886–8)

I.

*) for small hands: $\frac{5 5 4 5 5 5 4 2}{1 2 1 2 1 2 1 1}$

II.

III.

Un poco presto e con sentimento

IV.

END OF EDITION